Mrs. Carrie Warner Morehouse

The Legend of Psyche

And Other Verses

Mrs. Carrie Warner Morehouse

The Legend of Psyche
And Other Verses

ISBN/EAN: 9783337155643

Printed in Europe, USA, Canada, Australia, Japan

Cover: Foto ©Thomas Meinert / pixelio.de

More available books at **www.hansebooks.com**

CARRIE WARNER MOREHOUSE

THE LEGEND OF PSYCHE

AND OTHER VERSES

HOLIDAY EDITION

ST. JOHNSBURY
CHARLES T. WALTER
1889

CONTENTS.

THE LEGEND OF PSYCHE.

THE LEGEND OF PSYCHE.

TAKE Fancy's pinions, and with me
Go through the air and o'er the sea,
Where, fair in all its beauty, lies
A land with blue and sunny skies.
There th' everlasting city, Rome,
Crowns seven hills with many a dome;
And at their feet there flows along
The yellow Tiber, famed in song.

O Rome! thy glory could not last,
Thou'rt but a shadow of the past.
Thy domes still heavenward lift their hands;
The Tiber flows o'er golden sands;

Thy hills still lift themselves on high,
And over all thy wondrous sky;
But broken shaft and ruined wall
Proclaim how great has been thy fall.

'Twas centuries ago, at Rome,
An humble sculptor had his home.
Before the works of master hands,
With quickened breath, he longing stands.
His very soul within him burns,
For power like theirs he eager yearns;
Then into forms like unto these,
His fingers mould the clay with ease.

At day-dawn, in the eastern sky,
All tinged with red the cloudlets lie,
And in the west, a glittering star,
That sends its quivering beams afar.

The sculptor's work of yesterday
The day-dawn star sees swept away ;
So few, alas ! its beauties seem,
Unlike the beauties of his dream.

Filled with a vague and restless pain,
The sculptor wanders forth again.
Before a garden's open gate,
His aimless feet a moment wait ;
The leaping fountains everywhere
With joyous music fill the air,
And blooming flowers and laden trees
Fling fragrance upon every breeze.

Near by the splashing fountain's side,
A maiden fair the sculptor spied,
With slender form and noble face —
A beauteous picture, full of grace.

A face that once had had a charm
To guide a master painter's arm ;
The face of Psyche, at which, dazed,
The sculptor yesterday had gazed.

He homeward turns with eager start,
The maiden's image in his heart,
And out of soft and yielding clay
The form of Psyche moulds, straightway.
And for the first time, with just pride,
He looks on his work, and is satisfied.
No longer vague and shadowy
His ideal is, but reality.

Within the yard, near by his door,
Had lain for twenty years or more,
A block of marble, soiled and gray
With the dust sifted o'er it, day by day,

But white within as drifted snow ;
From out this block should Psyche grow.
And the star of the morning understood,
It saw God's gift to the sculptor was good.

With careful hands, day after day,
The marble block is hewn away,
Until from out that piece of stone
The form of a beautiful girl has grown ;
A Psyche, so fair in every part,
It becomes enshrined in the sculptor's heart.
He now has the power for which he strove,
He now has learned that life is love.

The marble Psyche now complete,
He must the living Psyche meet ;
Must hear her voice, which on his ear
Like music fell, most sweet to hear.

Through the garden where the trees
Fill with perfume every breeze ;
By the fountains splashing there,
Filling with music the fragrant air ;

Through the lofty halls, the nobleman's
    pride,
Until he has reached the maiden's side.
To tell of the beautiful Psyche done
He vainly tries ; when scarce begun,
The sound of her voice, the touch of her
    hand,
Cause him to lose his self-command,
And scarcely knowing what he speaks;
His love he tells, and answer seeks.

But she, a maid of noble birth,
Deems such low love of little worth ;

With reddening cheek and flashing eye,
She bids him from her presence fly.
Like one who, wandering in his sleep,
His onward way can scarcely keep,
He staggers homeward ; night and day,
Unnoticed by him, pass away.

Through the cold gray light of the morn-
    ing skies,
The twinkling star saw him arise,
Trembling and shaking, from his bed,
Stand near the statue with bowed head ;
One yearning look on the face so dear,
Then he drags it to the garden near,
And soon the Psyche, so fair to behold,
Was hid from sight in the dark, damp
    mould.

3

The hours have lengthened into days;
Days into weeks; grim fever lays
The sculptor low and near to death;
Fainter grows his labored breath.
From a convent near a monk was sent,
To baffle death his will he lent,
With watchful care and words of cheer
Came health, and balm for the heart so
    drear.

To shun the ills which befall us here,
The sculptor sought the convent near.
At the evening hour, when the twilight fell,
He stood by the window of his cell,
Looked out o'er the city of old Rome.
Saw ruined wall and towering dome,
The yellow Tiber, flushed with rose,
And distant mountains, white with snows;

Into his heart there came a calm
Contentment, like a healing balm.
The seasons came; the seasons went;
Nature to each her beauty lent.
The morning star that watched so well
Pierced e'en the darkness of his cell;
Noticed, at last, his slow-drawn breath,
Then saw his eyes grow dim in death.

*   *   *   *   *   *

Three centuries had flown away,
And left alike growth and decay.
Where once had been the sculptor's home,
A stately convent reared its dome.
A gentle nun had passed away,
And in the yard, at dawn of day,
Her grave was dug; then, dazzling white,
A form of marble came in sight.

Into the rosy morning air
Was lifted out a Psyche fair,—
Glistening, pure, complete it stands,
As when it left its maker's hands.
Upon this Psyche fair men gazed,
In admiration lost; amazed
At the wondrous beauty of form and face.
But whose the hand had carved such grace?

None knew save the star, that from its
        throne
In the morning skies, shone out alone.
That glittering star which had watched so
        well,
Could the sculptor's life and sufferings tell.
His life with sin and sorrow stained
Was o'er, but the work of his hand re-
        mained:

But a form of stone in reality,
Yet a symbol of immortality.

OTHER VERSES.

SPRING'S BLOSSOMS.

Now fades away 'neath tall hedge-row
   Or pine, where sunlight never peers,
The last, long-lingering streak of snow,
   And fading wets the earth with tears, —

Warm tears, that wake to life the flowers
   Low sleeping, safe from Winter's breath ;
And joy and gladness fill the hours,
   For Life once more has conquered Death.

On river banks the willow sprout
   Is covered with a faint green mist,

4

And hangs its golden catkins out ;
  The maples blush, by sunbeams kissed.

Low 'mongst brown rifts of last year's green
  Where careless feet might tread on them
The sweet arbutus buds are seen ;
  The wind-flower nods on slender stem.

And every marshy nook is bright
  With yellow cups of marigold,
And soon, its face up to the light,
  The modest violet will hold.

A blossom here, a blossom there,
  Tells that the earth with Spring is rife,
And sounds of gladness fill the air,
  For Death once more gives way to Life.

MARGERY'S QUEST.

AFAR in the hazy distance,
  The mountains dim and blue ;
A stretch of ripening wheat fields,
  With breezes rippling through.

Nearer, the wide-spread meadows,
  With their fragrant heaps of hay ;
And, over all, the blue
  Of a cloudless summer day.

Maid Margery wanders slowly
  Adown a lane, near by,

With eager gaze she's seeking
  A four-leaf clover to spy.

And now she finds the treasure,
  And hides it in her shoe ;
And earnestly she wishes
  The hope of her heart prove true.

There are steps in the lane behind her,
  A form beside her own,
And a manly voice is speaking
  In an earnest, tender tone.

Needs not the charm of the clover
  Within her shoe concealed,
To bring to her wish the answer
  That the tone of his voice revealed.

Dim grow the distant mountains,
   The wheat fields are at rest,
And under the sky of evening
   Maid Margery ends her quest.

EDELWEISS.

On the lofty Alpine summits,
    Near the snow,
Where the weary-footed climbers
    Seldom go,

Grows a flower, so they tell me,
    Pure and white, —
Star-like blossoms, shooting up
    Into the light.

And throughout all Switzerland,
    Maidens know

How it came there, close to snow-land,
    Years ago.

Lived a maid, so runs the legend,
    Once on earth,
So pure that ne'er was found a suitor
    Of like worth.

And, at last, into a flower
    Like a star,
She was changed, and on the mountains
    Placed afar ;

Close beside the virgin whiteness
    Of the snow,—
Type of womanhood most lovely,
    Here below.

And the youth who to the maiden
    Whom he loves,
Brings the priceless star-like blossom,
    Worthy proves ;

For 'tis only through much peril
    And much pain,
One the edelweiss, that peerless
    Flower, may gain.

And, if the maiden in her girdle
    Place the flower,
The lover knows her heart is his
    From that hour.

TWO DAYS.

BRIGHT shone the sun in the morning,
  Not a cloud was seen in the sky,
Save here and there a tiny speck
  That floated lazily by.

In through the open window
  Came the faintly blowing breeze,
Bringing delicious fragrance
  From the full-blown apple trees.

Idly rocked the robin
  On the bough of an elm, near by,

5

And over the distant meadow
  Came the plover's mournful cry.

Blue were the distant mountains,
  Seen through the hazy air;
Throughout the realms of Nature
  Peace reigned everywhere.

*   *   *   *   *   *

Bright shone the sun in the morning,
  But clouds came in the sky,
And with even swifter motion
  They chase each other by.

Against the close-shut window
  Beats the wind, now loud, now low;

And the petals of the apple blooms
  Fall on the ground like snow.

Roughly the elm tree's branches
  Are tossing to and fro,
And the cry of the distant plover
  Sounds more like a cry of woe.

Hid are the distant mountains,
  By the fast on-coming rain;
The Storm King, in all his fury,
  Invades Nature's peaceful domain.

A LEGEND.

WHERE the waters of the Danube
  With a rippling current flow,
Walked a maiden and her lover,
  In the days of long ago.

Life to them was full of sweetness,
  All the earth seemed glad and gay,
Taking from their hearts its gladness; —
  The morrow was their wedding day.

On the river's bank, near by them,
  A modest bunch of flowerets grew,

Touching daintily the waters, —
  Tiny flowers of purest blue.

These tiny flowers the maiden saw,
  And, ever quick to do her pleasure,
The lover left the maiden's side,
  Eager to gain the wished-for treasure.

With willing hands the flowers he plucks,
  And thinks how well they'll grace the
      maid;
Beneath his feet the bank gives way, —
  Why from her side should he have
      strayed?

He tossed the flowers at her feet,
  O, the cold and cruel river!

"Vergiss mein nicht," he softly sighed,
  Then sank from out her sight forever.

And such the dreadful christening
  Those tiny flowers received that day ;
And ever since, forget-me-not
  Has been true love's own flower, alway.

A WINDOW PICTURE.

ENCLOSED within my window frame
 A fairer picture lies
Than artist's hand could e.... paint
 With all his magic dyes.

Broad fields, with daisies all abloom,
 Low hills, in greenness dressed;
While in the background, blue and dim,
 The mountains raise their crest.

A changing picture,—now the sun
 Lights all with mellow tint;

Then clouds, and over field and wood
   The darkening shadows glint.

Yet ever, midst the changing lights,
   The distant mountains tower,
Dimly outlined against the sky,
   In grandeur clothed, and power.

And thus my window picture lies,
   Changing, but ever fair;
For summer sun or summer cloud,
   But add new beauties there.

APPLE BLOSSOMS.

ONCE more a robe of soft, sweet green
Brightens the earth with tender sheen.

And where, on marsh and mountain side,
A golden mist was scattered wide,

With leaves of bright and vivid green
Every low bush and tree is seen.

From sunny South-land, winds of Spring
Blow soft, and life and gladness bring;

Causing the fields of verdant grass
To break in ripples as they pass,

6

While ev'ry leaflet, green and bright,
Quivers and shakes, as with delight.

Loosed at the South wind's gentle call,
In showers the apple blossoms fall,

And through my window, open wide,
Comes in their fragrance, like a tide.

O, sweet and fragrant breath of Spring!
What tender memories you bring

Of other days, so like to these,
When apple blossoms filled the trees!

Sweet memories, that wake to view
With each returning Spring, anew.

MAY FLOWERS.

Two centuries ago, and more,
   And o'er the stormy ocean wide,
The Pilgrims sought New England's shore,
   Where they their faith need no more hide.

When wooed by April's gentle showers,
   And fanned by softest breeze of May,
You showed your buds, O sweet May flow-
      ers !
   Strewn all about their woodland way,

Did ye not seem like flowers they knew
   In that far home beyond the sea?

Like hawthorn buds, whose beauty grew
  Most fair in month of May, like ye?

And when, throughout the wooded shore,
  Your fragrant breath filled all the air,
Ye must have brought sweet hope once
    more
  To hearts before filled with despair.

O sweetest of New England's flowers!
  Blooming when winter's sway is o'er,
Ye come, like rainbows after showers,
  God's promises to bring once more.

IN LATE SUMMER.

At drowsy noon the crickets sing,
   The days grow short, the nights are chill ;
The gleaming tints of Autumn creep
   Over the distant wooded hill.

The days grow short, the nights are chill,
   The thistle's down floats in the air,
The clematis, out-reaching, strives
   To make the roadside hedges fair.

The thistle's down floats in the air,
   Bright red the sumac berries glow ;

Where roses blushed or daisies bloomed,
   Tall scarlet lilies bend and blow.

Bright red the sumac berries glow,
   In every breeze the sunflowers nod,
And every wayside nook is bright
   With aster blooms and golden rod.

In every breeze the sunflowers nod, —
   O summer days, could you but last !
From the far distance comes the sound
   Of winter's cold and withering blast.

IF WE COULD KNOW.

DEAR friend of mine, if we could know
Which one of us the first would go, —
Would leave behind this earthly strand
And journey to the better land!

If it were you who first must go,
Leaving my heart to mourn you so!
Could I one moment lose from view
Your loving face, so good and true?

If it were I must leave behind,
All earthly ties that hold and bind!

Would you more often love express,
With earnest words of tenderness?

Beyond today that we should know
It is not best, — God wills it so ;
But whether it be you or me
Who first must cross that unknown sea,

God grant the time but short shall be
That separates you, dear, from me, —
Between the parting on this side,
And the sweet meeting 'cross the tide.

SIR GONDEBERT.

A LEGEND OF THE LILY.

In her proud castle, by the Rhine,
  Dwelt Lady Hildegarde;
'Mongst all the Knights Sir Gondebert
  Was first in her regard.

When with his knights he rode away
  To war in the Holy Land,
He wore a banner broidered o'er
  By Hildegarde's fair hand.

With lilies, golden, white, and red,
  Upon an azure field,

7

And he who bore that banner forth
   Could ne'er in battle yield.

But time passed on, no tidings came
   To the lady from her Knight,
And long she mourned him 'mongst the
     slain
   Or captured, in the fight.

A noble baron long had wooed
   And sued her for her hand,
And so, at last, fair Hildegarde
   Yielded to his demand.

But ere the bridal, Hildegarde
   Her trusty maiden sent,

And bade her watch from the highest tower,
　For a banner, lily sprent.

E'en as they stood before the priest,
　And he was murmuring low
The words that soon should make them one,
　The maiden ran below.

"I see a knight's train coming on,
　His pennon borne before,
With lilies, red and white and gold,
　It is embroidered o'er."

"It is my knight," cried Hildegarde,
　"To whom I pledged my love;
And I will marry none but him,
　Oh! help me, God above."

And so it was Sir Gondebert
  At last had won his bride,
And ever from their donjon-tower
  That banner floated wide.

And as, upon the gentle winds,
  The banner fell and rose,
It waved a welcome to its friends,
  A menace to its foes.

THE ROBIN'S NEST.

THE robin sang with a saddened heart,
  "Why tarries the Spring so long?
I never shall fly to my nest again,
  The apple-blooms among."

The leafless tree, in the wintry wind,
  Mournfully swayed and sighed;
"Ah! never again will the robin's nest
  Among my branches hide."

But the kindly Spring, with its balmy
      breath,
  Covered the tree with flowers;

And the robin's nest 'mong its branches hid
All through the summer hours.

TRAILING ARBUTUS.

ALL Winter long earth's robes have been
    Of sombre hue, or purest white;
But with the Spring, lo! everything
    Grows fresh and green from sheer de-
      light.

From April skies fall plenteous showers,
    Rich boons from out a generous hand;
And balmy breezes from the South
    Bring new life to the waiting land.

The withered leaves are swept aside,
    Once Autumn's pride, now dry and sere,

And nestled low 'mong leaves of green
  The sweet arbutus flowers appear.

O blushing blossoms of the Spring,
  Breathing sweet perfume on the air!
To those who listen ye may teach
  A lesson, grand as ye are fair.

In life's dark ways we oft may find
  Blessings unknown, but pure and sweet,
If we will only brush aside
  The withered leaves beneath our feet.

THE ERLKING.

FROM THE GERMAN OF GOETHE.

WHO rides so late, through a night so wild?
It is a father with his child;
He has the boy close in his arm,
He holds him safe, he keeps him warm.

"My son, why so timidly hide thine eye?"
"See'st thou not, father, the Erlking nigh?
The Erlenking, with train and crown?"
"I see but a streak of mist, my son."

"Thou charming child, come, go with me!
E'en beautiful games will I play with thee;

8

With many gay flowers the strand is sown,
My mother has many a golden gown."

"My father, my father, and dost thou not
    hear
What the Erlking whispers so soft in my
    ear?"
"Be quiet, stay quiet, my own dear child!
The dry leaves are rustling this night so
    wild."

"Wilt thou, pretty boy, go with me?
My daughters shall nobly wait on thee.
My daughters the nightly revels keep,
They'll rock thee, and dance, and sing thee
    to sleep."

"My father, my father, and sees't thou not
    there
The Erlking's daughters in gloomy air?"
"My son, my son, I look close that way,
I see but the willows, old and gray."

"I love thee, thy beauty charms my sight,
And art thou not willing, then will I use
    might."
"My father, my father, hold close your
    arm,
The Erlenking has done me harm."

The father shudders, he rides on fast,
The sobbing child in his arms close clasped;
He reaches the yard with toil and dread,
For in his arms his child lies dead.

GOOD NIGHT.

Good night, good night, the day is done;
Low in the west has sunk the sun,
Like lamps set in the summer sky,
The twinkling stars shine out on high.
Upon the roofs of the quiet town
The full pale moon shines calmly down.
Their branches swayed by every breeze,
Sentinel-like, loom up the trees,
Casting weird shadows o'er the street
Where all day long passed busy feet.
Hushed and at rest all Nature seems,
Inviting quiet sleep and dreams.

He who doth note the sparrow's fall,
Keeps tender watch over us all ;
So, till the rosy morning light,
Sleep peacefully.   Good night, good night.

COMPENSATION.

WHERE yesterday the crested waves
   Dashed on the sandy shore,
Are only rocks and clinging grass, —
   And hushed the sea's deep roar.

All night waiting the punctual tide
   The patient shore has lain,
Sure, with the coming morning light, ·
   The tide will turn again.

All day the sky may be dull and gray,
   With never the sun's clear light,

And all the night the heavy clouds
   May hide the stars from sight;

But the sun will surely shine again,
   And all the clouds will flee,
And the stars send out their twinkling light
   O'er all the land and sea.

And life, at times, seems full of care,
   And only brings us pain;
But patient wait, the cares shall flee,
   And loss shall sure bring gain.

Ebb-tide and flood, darkness and light,
   The bitter with the sweet, —
God metes them out in portions just,
   And so makes life complete.

A WINTER LEGEND.

FROM THE GERMAN OF ECKLEMANN.

Now sleeps the earth!   With Winter's veil
  Of white she is concealed from view;
She is not dead, but sleeping, hushed
  Till Spring again shall wake anew.

As the little child, without a fear,
  Lies nestled close to its mother's breast,
So, hidden on the breast of earth
  Lie the flower-children, lulled to rest.

And there they dream of breezes wild,
  Of warm sunshine, and sparkling dews;

Entranced with odors sweet they see
    Green woods, and meads of many hues.

They listen, and hear the songs of birds,
    And what the waves on the brooklet say ;
They prattle with the butterflies ;
    The bees buzz by, and say "Good day !"

The flowerets stretch themselves on high
    To see the splendor far and near ;
The beautiful dream is vanished now,
    And see, — the Spring is really here.

9

IN MEMORY.

'T is only some pink-tinged blossoms
  I hold within my hand,
That come when the breath of Spring-time
  Gladdens all the land ;
Blooms of the May-flower, pure and sweet,
That I picked 'mong the leaves beneath my
  feet.

Only some pink-tinged blossoms,
  But their fragrance, like a key,
Has opened the doors of mem'ry,
  And let such sad thoughts free, —

Thoughts of the Spring-times, years gone
    by,
When we were together, she and I.

The air is full of odors,
  Oh, the breath of Spring is sweet!
Blue are the skies above me,
  Blossoms are round my feet;
But oh! these joyous days of Spring
Can ne'er to my heart any gladness bring.

She loved these sweet May blossoms,
  And hastened the first to seek;
The dainty pink of their petals
  But reflected the blush on her cheek.
Ah, me! the days are long and drear,
Now that dear face is no longer here,

I cannot wish her back here
  In this world of sin and pain,
For her are joys immortal,
  For me life's griefs remain;
But, oh! when the bloom and fragrance
    abound,
My heart mourns over a grass-grown
    mound.

LOVES ME, LOVES ME NOT.

Maiden with the winsome face,
Moving slowly, but with grace
Through the daisies and the grass,
Plucking handfuls as you pass,

Tell me why across thy face
Flit the shadows, out of place;
Why those eyes are downward cast,
Hardly heeding what is passed.

"Loves me, loves me not," she said,
Scarcely lifting up her head;

And the petals of the flower
Fall about her in a shower.

"Does he love me, daisy? tell!
For I love him, oh, so well.
Will he love me, daisy? say!
I would wait, ah, many a day."

Slowly drop the petals down,
Falling, fluttering, one by one.
Can the daisy tell? ah me, 'tis dumb!
But thou shalt know in the days to come.

A MEMORY.

Do you remember those summer days
   That we spent on an isle in the sea ;
Those days of whose full happiness
   Naught remains but a memory?
Oh ! it seemed like some enchanted isle,
   Afar from the great world's strife ;
And to watch the waves and the flitting sails,
   Seemed peace enough for life.

Do you remember the southern shore,
   Where we whiled away many an hour ;
And the pathway cut in the solid rock,
   The mark of some wondrous power?

Oh! sweet was the song of the ceaseless
    waves,
  As they lapped the rocks alway;
But after a storm with an angry roar,
  They dashed on the rocks in spray.

Do you remember those moonlight sails,
  And the glittering waves of the sea;
And the glimmering light in the lighthouse
    tower,
  So far from you and me?
Oh! the moonlit ripples soft music made,
  And the boat with its sail agleam,
Seemed to float away to an unknown world,
  On the path of the moon's bright beam.

Do you remember the friends we met
  In that summer long gone by;

And the happy hours together spent,
  So free from care or sigh?
Oh! the friends of those pleasant summer
    days
  Perchance we'll meet no more,
Until we have crossed the sea of time,
  And stand on eternity's shore.

10

ALONE.

Pleasant were those bygone days,
  Days in the summer weather,
When, side by side, we wandered on
  Adown life's way together.

Verdure and bloom on every side,
  Fragrance in the air,
The song-bird calling to its mate, —
  Ah! life seemed wondrous fair.

Leafless and bare, the branches now
  Are swaying in the breeze,

No flower-fragrance in the air,
  No bird-songs from the trees.

O'er all the land grim Winter has
  His chilly mantle thrown,
And down life's cold and cheerless way
  I sadly walk alone.

THE MAPLE TREE'S LAMENT.

"Wooed by the gentle spring-time winds,
  My buds of glossy sheen
Burst forth, and soon my top was crowned
  With leaves of brightest green.

"All summer long my heart was glad,
  For the birds flew in and out,
And 'mong my branches, spreading wide,
  They built their nests about.

"October came with its pleasant days,
  And yet with a breath so keen

That it turned to brilliant red and gold
  My leaves of beautiful green.

" And soon they left me, one by one,
  Joining the earth's damp mould;
And Winter kindly cover'd them o'er
  With a mantle white and cold.

" And now, a bare and leafless tree,
  I stand in the chilling blast,
And the empty nests among my boughs
  Tell only of joys that are past."

O maple tree! with gladness hear
  The tidings that I bring;
There yet shall come, in His own time,
  Another wonderful Spring.

Thy buds shall then once more grow green,
   And crown thee as before,
And the birds fly out, and the birds fly in,
   As they did in days of yore.

THE BROOKLET.

FROM THE GERMAN OF GOETHE.

THOU brooklet, silver-bright and clear,
Thou ever hastenest past me here
Upon thy bank.   I wonder how
Thou camest here?   Where goest thou?

From the bosom dark of the rock came I;
O'er flower and moss my course doth lie;
Floating upon my mirror true
Is the picture of the heavenly blue.

Therefore my mind is free as air;
I am driven forth, I know not where:

But He who called me from the stone
Will never let my way be lone.

HARRY'S JOURNEY.

Come, now, my five-year old,
  The sun has said good night,
A long way you must travel
  Before to-morrow's light.

Your head is growing weary,
  Your eyes begin to wink;
Ah me! that funny sand-man
  Has been this way, I think.

We'll put on your white "dream dress,"
  And place you in your boat,

11

Then out on the Drowsy river
   To the sea of Sleep you'll float, —

Float along so gently
   To the beautiful Land of Dreams,
And there your boat will anchor
   Till to-morrow's sunlight beams.

A pleasant journey, Harry,
   Across the sea of Sleep;
He who doth note the sparrows
   His kind watch o'er thee keep!

ONLY A VIOLET.

In a little shaded nook,
Where a rippling, gurgling brook
Flowed, with many a bend and crook,
    A modest floweret grew.
The bright blue skies up overhead
Reflected from the brooklet's bed;
The floweret, hanging o'er its head,
    Grew of the same bright hue.

Its fragrant breath filled all the air,
Making the summer days more fair;
Its beauty was beyond compare—
    This modest flower of blue.

Its hiding place was never known,
It bloomed and faded all alone,
And yet, the world had fairer grown,
    Because the violet grew.

O heart, whose life seems lone and drear,
Be patient, and of better cheer,
And you will find a lesson here
    From this flower of heavenly hue.
Thy life seems worthless and obscure,
Yet thou, by living true, most sure
Canst shed around a sweetness pure,
    E'en as the violet blue.

THE MESSAGE ON THE WIRES.

My path, one early winter's day,
O'er a country roadside lay,
Just where the winds came sweeping down
Between the hills, beyond the town.

First on the left, then on the right,
Tall, towering poles rose in their might,
Their arms outreaching to uphold
The wires that stretched for miles untold.

Just then the winds came sweeping down
Between the hills, beyond the town,

And music rose, now soft, now sharp,
Like notes from an Æolian harp.

So soft and low, so sweet and clear,
The notes that fell upon my ear,
Methought the wires broke into song
Because of thoughts they bore along.

Perchance the word from some dear friend,
That days of waiting soon would end,
And those between whom seas had rolled,
Should greet each other, as of old.

Just then the wires, swept by the gale,
Gave forth a long and piercing wail,
As if the message borne along
Caused sighs of pain in place of song.

And now, methought, to some poor heart
Flies news that bitter tears will start—
Perchance some face they've loved to greet,
They never more on earth will meet.

O magic wires, that o'er the land
Your meshes weave on every hand!
Wondrous your power, for in a breath,
You sing of life, or sigh o'er death.

The swift-winged words you bear along
Cause hearts to break forth into song;
Or to some life, with sudden blow,
You bring the words of death and woe.

A FADED ROSE.

FROM THE GERMAN.

TURNING o'er the leaves of a book,
   A faded rosebud met my eye,
Pale and dead, like her whose hand
   Had gathered it in days gone by.

Ah! more and more on the evening breeze
   Her memory dies, and soon I know
My life will end; I, too, shall be   .
   As pale as she who loved me so.

ONLY AN EMPTY NEST.

ONLY an empty nest,
   High in a leafless tree,
Where the wailing winds pass by,
   With a mournful melody.

Only an empty nest,
   Swept by the wintry blast,
Telling of days gone by,
   And joys that could not last.

But faith looks far away
   Through the drifting snow and sleet,

12

Almost catches the sound
  Of swift on-coming feet ;

Knows that the leafless limbs
  With verdure shall be crowned,
And the happy songs of birds
  Throughout the air resound.

THE OLD AND THE NEW.

Janus-like, between the parting
   And the coming guest we stand,
Bidding farewell to the Old Year,
   Reaching to the New our hand.

Old Year, thou art tried and faithful,
   Dearly loved by every heart;
Yet, to friends so true and trusty,
   Sometimes comes the time to part.

New Year, thou art as a stranger,
   Yet with joy we welcome thee;

Fraught with blessings without number,
May thy coming to us be.

LIFE'S SEASONS.

WHAT do these flitting seasons bring,
  The seasons of life's year?
The Spring, with blossoms thick for fruit,
  Brings hope of after-cheer.

The Summer brings the sunny days;
  Life's pulse beats fast and high:
And clouds that briefly hide from view
  The deep blue of the sky.

The Autumn brings the ripened fruit;
  The full corn in the ear;

The glowing color, token sure
   Of the dying of life's year.

The Winter brings the cold, gray sky ;
   Bright hopes of long ago
'Neath drifting snows lie buried now,
   But Spring will come, we know.

A DREAM-SONG.

A VOLUME bound in white and gold
   I held within my hand,
And o'er and o'er, with eager eyes,
   The rhythmic lines I scanned.

Verses from a brave woman's heart,
   If haply he might take
Whose weary soul was all athirst,
   And here his thirst might slake.

Night came, and over all the world
   Her sable curtains flung,

Yet e'en in sleep those rhythmic lines,
   Through all my pulses rung.

Of that God-given, wondrous power
   I seemed to be possessed,
And through my mind flashed line on line,
   In choicest words expressed.

Yet once again the rhythmic lines
   In sweetest cadence flow.
Oh! can it be that power is mine
   Which I have longed to know?

Morning, at last, with dewy feet,
   Threw wide the gates of day.
Alas! my dream-song, like the night,
   Had vanished quite away.

BABY'S CHRISTMAS GIFT.

WHAT shall we give to the baby, —
  Our baby just one year old?
She wouldn't know about Christmas,
  Not even if she were told.

You may hang up her little stockings
  Where Santa will surely see,
Or put all sorts of playthings
  Upon the Christmas tree, —

But what does she know about Santa
  And his wonderful midnight ride,

13

Or the tree that bears such fruitage
  Only at Christmas-tide?

She'd only look in wonder
  From out her big, blue eyes,
And reach her hand for the playthings
  With innocent surprise.

So kisses sweet without number,—
  Kisses and love untold—
These we will give to the baby,
  Our baby, just one year old.

www.ingramcontent.com/pod-product-compliance
Lightning Source LLC
Chambersburg PA
CBHW031441270326
41930CB00007B/822